Sèvres

COLLECTORS' BLUE BOOKS

Sèvres

CARL CHRISTIAN DAUTERMAN

STUDIO VISTA, LONDON

To F. L. S. and I. E. L.

FRONTISPIECE: Vincennes ewer. Ca. 1750. 9¾ in high. Museum of Fine Arts, Boston, Forsyth Wickes Collection.

SBN 289 79722 5

Published in London 1970 by Studio Vista Ltd, Blue Star House, Highgate Hill, London N19

Printed in the United States of America
Jacket designed by Joseph Bourke Del Valle
Book designed by the Bert Clarke Design Group

FIG. I Vincennes dish with view of château at Vincennes. Ca. 1745–1750. Musée National de Céramique, Sèvres.

THE PORCELAIN OF SÈVRES is a continuing symbol of old France. An extravagance of kings during its early years, it survived the downfall of Louis XVI, weathered the lean decade that followed, and regained its glamour under Napoleon. During the succeeding century and a half, it has adjusted to the vicissitudes of politics, esthetics and economics. Today it is, like Wedgwood in England, a forward-looking enterprise that continues to be mindful of its own tradition. Originating at Vincennes in 1738–1740, the manufacture was moved to Sèvres, a suburb to the southwest of Paris, in 1756. Although in general application the term Sèvres comprehends the porcelain made at both places, a special cachet attaches to the name Vincennes. The reason is that it refers not only to the place of origin, but also connotes a medium invested with the vigor of the full Rococo and the experimental freshness of a new enterprise.

During the reign of Louis XV (1723–1774) when this venture was launched, France was the acknowledged leader in the arts among the nations of Europe. Circumstances, including the intervention of the Crown, soon burdened the infant manufactory with the responsibility of creating and maintaining standards worthy of Europe's most sophisticated court. It is the purpose of this little book to illustrate how the mastery over a difficult medium made it possible for the new porcelain to assume its place with furniture and goldsmiths' work at the forefront of the decorative arts of France.

The origin of Sèvres is traceable to the experiments of two runaways from the porcelain factory at Chantilly. Appearing at Vincennes in 1738, Robert and Gilles Dubois boasted of their familiarity with the mysteries of making porcelain. Their claims induced visions of wealth and prestige, but the results were in all probability rather negligible, as in their previous roles the brothers had been a turner and a painter, respectively.[1] By 1741 the prospect for success shifted to François Gravant, a onetime maker of faience (and a green-

1. E. S. Auscher, *A History and Description of French Porcelain*, London: Cassell & Co., 1905, p. 44.

grocer!). Gravant had somehow acquired the "arcanum," or secret, of the materials and processes for making porcelain. He received the support of Orry de Fulvy, comptroller of finance. This official arranged to provide funds, possibly including some from the king himself, and also to give the enterprise a home in the Château of Vincennes, on the outskirts of Paris.

It was not until 1745, however, that a syndicate was formed for the purpose of manufacturing porcelain on a commercial scale. Its privilege, signed by the king, specified that the purpose of the organization was to make a ceramic in imitation of Saxon (Meissen) porcelain, *i.e.*, employing colored grounds with decorative reserves and gilding. The organization was put on a business-like footing, backed by leading financiers, most of whom were concession-aires known quaintly as "farmers of the taxes." Its titular head was Machault, the king's finance minister, whose representative on the job was Jacques-René Boileau de Picardie, a shrewd administrator. The color chemist was Jean Hellot, a metallurgist and member of the Academy of Sciences. Jean-Claude Duplessis, chief designer of vessels and their bronze mounts, was lent from the staff of the king, as was the court painter Jean-Adam Matthieu, an enameler. Artists of the caliber of Boucher and Oudry advised and contrib-uted decorative themes. Gravant, the former greengrocer of Chantilly, con-trolled the preparation of the paste and glaze, for which he received a royalty on all the porcelain sold.

The enterprise grew. By 1749 nearly a hundred people were employed, according to de Fulvy.[2] In spite of its gifted staff, however, the factory never made enough money to keep profits ahead of expenses. In 1747 the king pro-vided a subsidy of 40,000 livres, and added 30,000 more during each of the next two years. In an effort to stem the tide of debts, Machault arranged that the factory be given a share of the fees from the hallmarking of silver and gold, as well as the taxes on all the candle wax sold in Paris. But this measure also proved insufficient. At various times the monarch bought blocks of shares in the enterprise, until he became its sole proprietor in 1759. Indeed, he also served as its most effective salesman, as did his successor, Louis XVI. At the turn of each year, between Christmas and Epiphany, exhibitions were held either at Versailles or at the Louvre, with the king himself selling the porcelain (even setting the prices, it is said). The prices were high, and it was not regarded as good diplomacy for ladies and gentlemen of the court to

2. *Ibid.*

abstain from making purchases. Louis XVI was so enthusiastic about his porcelain exhibitions that he once refused to wait for the workmen, unpacked things himself, breaking some and getting services all mixed up.

It should be remembered that Vincennes-Sèvres was not the earliest porcelain produced in France. Rouen and St. Cloud had claimed success in the last decade of the seventeenth century. The early years of Louis XV saw the creation of factories at Chantilly (1725) and Mennecy (1734). The porcelain of Vincennes-Sèvres shared with these a similar basic formula, and all the pieces produced in these factories belong to a category called, for want of a better name, soft-paste or "artificial" porcelain. They were the precursors in France of a true hard-paste porcelain, but not its technical equivalent.

It was outside France, at Meissen in Saxony (now part of East Germany), that a true hard paste was first produced in Europe. A few brief remarks about Meissen should be helpful at this point, as that factory provides the major yardstick for a comparison with Sèvres. Meissen was the first European producer of a porcelain compounded entirely of natural clays and minerals. Such porcelain was more practical to manufacture than earlier types, as its ingredients required less preparation and the paste was less prone to warp or fissure during firing. Losses from these faults were exasperatingly high among the soft pastes, owing in part to a lack of cohesiveness in the medium. The acceptability of Meissen's hard-paste formula was probably increased by a psychological factor: it was the technical counterpart of Chinese porcelain, demand for which had long exceeded the supply.

The essential ingredients of hard paste in the formula used by the Chinese and later at Meissen are china clay (kaolin) and china stone (pegmatite). The latter, which the Chinese call petuntse, is a rock containing feldspar and quartz. Both china stone and china clay are extracted directly from nature; they are not artificial compounds. The soft paste of Sèvres, on the other hand, was based essentially on a compound known to potters as "frit," which is manufactured by combining sand, soda, alum, saltpeter and plaster of Paris. This artificial product, actually a kind of glass, was reduced to a fine powder and mixed with whiting (pulverized chalk that has been washed) and marl (an earthy deposit, chiefly of clay and calcium carbonate). These constituted the paste, or porcelain mixture, which was not ready to be used, however, until it had been made workable by the addition of boiling water, glue and green soap. The resulting porcelain was thus chemically distinct from "true" or hard-paste porcelain. It differed also in its glaze, which contained lead oxide and could be quite thick, in contrast to the feldspathic glaze of Meissen, which was characteristically thin.

The porcelains of France continued to be of the soft-paste type for a long time after the first Saxon porcelain appeared on the market in 1710, in spite of Meissen's rapid domination of the European scene as a producer of hard paste. This situation invested Sèvres with another mission: that of competing with Meissen to wrest from it as much as possible of a lucrative market with a seemingly insatiable appetite for porcelain. In this task the innate genius of Sèvres was aided by an external event of immense significance: the Seven Years' War, during which Saxon Meissen suffered the setback of Prussian occupation under Frederick the Great. It was precisely in 1756 that Sèvres moved into its spacious new quarters, which, incidentally, included an apartment for the king. And it was during these years that the manufactory released a succession of inspired original shapes, including some that were decorated with a rose ground that became the envy of *porcelainiers* all over Europe. Before the end of the reign of Louis XV, Sèvres emerged as the most highly esteemed porcelain, the leader of fashion in its field. Fittingly, its soft-paste type was called *Porcelaine de France* in court circles and abroad.

One may well marvel that Sèvres was able to achieve such success while clinging to the use of the old-fashioned soft-paste formula. During the period from 1740 to 1770 many newly created factories followed Meissen's example in adopting the kaolinic type, but Sèvres did not abandon its obsolescent and uneconomical glassy frit until 1804. In the meantime, however, it produced another surprise: it entered into the manufacture, jointly, of hard and soft paste. The new formula was not released commercially until 1772. Collectors often are unfamiliar with the fact that hard paste did not immediately replace the older medium, and that Sèvres was probably unique among Continental factories in producing both kinds of porcelain concurrently for the remainder of the eighteenth century.

The story of hard paste in France is strongly colored by the affairs of the Hannong family. It begins with Charles-François Hannong, who owned a faience factory at Strasbourg and had at one time manufactured tobacco pipes. Presumably his work with white pipe clay led him to experiment with making "table porcelains." As early as 1726 he claimed to have given a service of forty-one pieces of porcelain to his guild. Whether this gift was actually porcelain or some species of porcelaneous material may never be established.

Other claims were made by that celebrated man of science René Antoine Ferchault de Réaumur, who experimented with a modification of the Chinese porcelain formula (which had become known in Europe through the letters of a Jesuit missionary, Père d'Entrecolles). Réaumur used talc and glass in place of kaolin and petuntse, in the belief that the Chinese word kaolin was to be interpreted as talc. The *Mémoires de l'Academie des Sciences* for 1727, 1729 and 1739 contain reports of his "new species of porcelain," which was adjudged by later generations to be a kind of devitrified glass.

The name of Hannong reentered the picture about 1752, when Charles' son Paul-Antoine was producing porcelain of the German type at Strasbourg, with the aid of kaolin and workers imported from across the Rhine. Vincennes, now backed by an enlarged syndicate, requested that his production be halted. In so doing, it was invoking its right to be the sole French producer of porcelain in the Meissen manner. Hannong appealed to the comptroller general, Machault, claiming exemption on the grounds that Strasbourg was a free town; the appeal was denied. In a crafty move, Vincennes offered to pay the expenses of two Strasbourg specialists if they would come to demonstrate their process. Reluctantly, Hannong sent his men, hoping in this way to gain a concession. The demonstration went well, and Hannong was given assurances of financial reward if he would reveal his formula. This he agreed to do in 1753, but in spite of a formalized contract, no payment was made. Instead, he was advised during the following year that Vincennes had secured an order that he demolish his kilns. The Vincennes organization took the position that the agreement had been nullified by Hannong's failure to provide a reliable French source of kaolin. The promised reward did not materialize until 1781, by which time Paul had died; a greatly reduced settlement was arranged with his son, Joseph-Adam. In the meantime, Paul had found more fertile soil in the Palatinate region of Germany, where the Elector Karl Theodore provided him with a new factory; thus in 1755 the Frankenthal porcelain factory was born.

The above account is only the sketchiest outline of France's participation in the race for *pâte dure*. While interest in this material was very high indeed at Vincennes-Sèvres, there was always a reluctance to make a beginning without being assured of an unlimited supply of kaolin within the national boundaries. So it was that, while an earlier start might have been made, it was not until 1768 that the operation became feasible, through the discovery of sizable deposits at Saint-Yrieix. Immediate success was achieved with the use of this material, and by 1772, as has been said, Sèvres launched into the commercial production of the new paste while still continuing with the old. The supply of kaolin here in the hills of Limousin proved to be so vast that it has continuously provided not only distant Sèvres but also the porcelain kilns that began to burgeon at nearby Limoges. (See Appendix for nineteenth- and twentieth-century pastes.)

Above: FIG. 3   Monteith. Date-marked for 1785. 5 × 11⅝ in. Mr. and Mrs. Charles B. Wrightsman Collection, New York.

Opposite: FIG. 2   Cup and saucer. Date-marked for 1770. Sterling and Francine Clark Art Institute, Williamstown.

FIG. 4　Apple-green tureen for stew. Date-marked for 1756. 11¾ in. high. Museum of
Fine Arts, Boston, Forsyth Wickes Collection.

CHAPTER I

Useful Wares

IN A SURVEY OF THE PRODUCTS of Vincennes-Sèvres, it is convenient to divide them into five categories.

Like that of any porcelain manufactory, the history of Sèvres is largely concerned with the production of articles for use on the table. Such "bread-and-butter" wares were essential to the economic health of the factory, constituting its major source of income. They were, for their day, mass-produced, in that molds and decorative patterns were used with considerable repetition. Yet so consummate was the mastery of potting and painting that we look upon the products today as objects of art rather than manufacture.

There is a special appropriateness, therefore, to the dish in Figure 1. It is decorated with a view of the original factory located in the Château at Vincennes, a town on the eastern edge of Paris. The new shapes and schemes of decoration emerging from Vincennes blossomed into the style called Sèvres. The earliest Vincennes porcelains took full advantage of the warm, almost organic whiteness of the material, using it as an ideal foil for limited decoration in color. Within a surprisingly short time, however, a tendency to cover large areas with solid color asserted itself: evidence, no doubt, of the avowed determination to create porcelain in the image of Meissen.

One of the most readily observable aspects of this porcelain is the extensive variety of articles it offered for the table. These are so numerous and in some instances so highly specialized as to reflect many nuances of eighteenth-century dining. For example, tureens of oval section were intended for soup, while matching tureens of round section were meant for *oglio* (Fig. 4), presumably a kind of stew. Other refinements were asparagus dishes, mustard pots, sauce cups, cheese dishes, chestnut bowls, ice cream cups with saucers, and condiment dishes in the form of three clustered baskets, their arched handles tied with a ribbon bowknot. There was also a range of cooling vessels— for fruit, for wine bottles of several sizes, and a *verrière* for wineglasses (Fig. 3). And the list is by no means exhausted.

Large services, many of them made to special order for royalty, form an impressive group among the useful wares. In their colors and variety of decoration they offer a cross section of the chief stylistic trends during the second half of the eighteenth century. One of the earliest was made for Louis XV as a gift to the Empress Maria Theresa in 1758. Its one hundred and eighty-five pieces were beautifully painted with festoons of green ribbons garlanded with flowers on a white ground, the major pieces enhanced with trophies and pairs of cherubs.

Among the better-known services are those made for Catherine the Great of Russia, Madame DuBarry, and the Cardinal Prince Louis de Rohan, whose role in the "affair of the diamond necklace" earned him the nickname Le Cardinal Collier. The Rohan service (Fig. 7) was made in 1772. It constituted part of the trappings of state for the prince while he was ambassador to Spain, and was obviously intended to impress his guests at official dinners. Its ground color is a limpid turquoise blue (called rather confusingly *bleu céleste*), interrupted by medallions of colorful tropical birds and overlaid with elaborate gilded foliation. The centers of the plates display Rohan's monogram in two tones of gilding, wreathed in a circle of oak leaves. The service consisted of three hundred and sixty pieces, and has been widely dispersed in a series of recent sales.

Madame DuBarry's service of 1770–1771 (Fig. 8) is in feminine taste, its white border decorated with garlands and blue vase forms called *cassolettes*. The monogram consists of the script letter *D* in gilding interlinked with a *B* composed of miniature blossoms. The set comprised three hundred and twenty items. Twelve soup plates are now in the Museum of Fine Arts, Boston; other important pieces are at the National Museum of Ceramics, Sèvres, and the Victoria and Albert Museum, London.

Much less feminine but eminently regal is the service made for Catherine the Great in 1778–1779. This was one of the largest services in the annals of Sèvres, containing a basic six hundred and sixteen pieces, to which a coffee service and other accessories were added, for a total of seven hundred and forty-four. Made of hard-paste porcelain, and decorated in a pronounced Neo-

COLOR PLATE I: Pair of bulb pots, apparently unique. Probably intended as samples of background color, patterns of gilding and subject matter of reserves. Ca. 1760. 6 in. high. Museum of Fine Arts, Boston, Forsyth Wickes Collection.

classical vein, it typifies the replacement of Rococo lightheartedness by the disciplined balance and Classical allusions fashionable during the reign of Louis XVI. Against a field of fluctuating turquoise blue is the empress' monogram, a crowned E (for Ekaterina) made of flowerettes and incorporating the Roman numeral II. The monogram dominates a design of profile heads and mythological scenes painted to simulate brown and white sardonyx cameos.

A set of original watercolor studies representing six or more alternatives is preserved at Sèvres. It illustrates the painstaking effort invested in the formulation of a design that Catherine would find acceptable. Apparently the drawings accompanied one or more examples of porcelain executed from the design thought by the art director to be most suitable. The Czarina seems to have chosen the one illustrated in Figure 5. This meticulous preparation parallels the practice of contemporary furniture makers, who sometimes made numerous drawings, then minature models, followed by full-scale models of substitute materials, in order to get the final approval of their clients before rather than after executing important commissions.

A service commissioned by Marie Antoinette is in a related vein, though employing animal motives because intended for use at her *laiterie* at Rambouillet (Fig. 6).

A delightful palette of colors was developed within the first few years: a deep blue (*bleu lapis*) and a lively turquoise blue (*bleu céleste*), in 1753; a soft yellow (*jaune jonquille*), about the same time; apple green (*vert pomme*), in 1756; and violet (*violette*) in 1757. The color most envied by other porcelain makers, however, was a subtle rose possessing a remarkable quality of freshness. This was called in later times "rose Pompadour," after the marquise who exercised such a strong influence upon the growth of the factory and the general development of the arts in France. The color was at its best (COLOR PLATE I) from the time of its appearance in 1758 until the death of the marquise in 1764. Revivals of it were attempted during the late seventies, but with less agreeable results. Its decline is further attributed to the death in 1775 of its inventor, a flower

Above: FIG. 5   Oval platter with turquoise blue borders, from the service of Catherine the Great. Date-marked for 1778. 13 in. long. Museum of Fine Arts, Boston, Forsyth Wickes Collection.

Below: FIG. 6   Cup and saucer from the service of Marie Antoinette. Date-marked for 1788. Musée National de Céramique, Sèvres.

Above: FIG. 7   Pair of plates with turquoise blue borders from the dessert service of Prince de Rohan. 1771–1772. 9¾ in. Mr. and Mrs. Charles B. Wrightsman Collection, New York. Below: FIG. 8   Soup plate from the dinner service of Mme du Barry. At right are the marks on underside of plate: factory mark with date letter s for 1771 and initials LB for Le Bel *jeune*. 9½ in. Museum of Fine Arts, Boston, Forsyth Wickes Collection.

painter named Xhrouet (or Xhrowet) who had succeeded in making it from a compound of gold; he undoubtedly supervised its preparation during his lifetime. A slight mystery surrounds the earliest use of rose Pompadour, in that while it is found on objects date-marked for 1757, there is no record of their sale before the end of 1758. It has been presumed that the color was not released until approved by the king, who may have held it in reserve to mark the thirty-seventh birthday of La Pompadour on December 29 of that year.

To achieve the full brilliance and sparkle so characteristic of Sèvres, it was necessary to face the hazards of two separate firings: the first at a high temperature to give the clay strength and permanence; the second to affix the coating of glaze, the colored enamels of the painted decoration and the gilding.[3] During the second firing the temperature had to be most delicately controlled. The technical mastery involved here, before the invention of precise devices for measuring high temperatures, made the kiln master's responsibility awesome indeed.

3. *Les Grands Services de Sèvres*, eds. Serge Grandjean and Marcelle Brunet, Paris: Musée National de Céramique de Sèvres, 1951, p. 16.

FIG. 9   Platter for tureen. 1771–1772. 18 in. long. Mr. and Mrs. Charles B. Wrightsman Collection, New York.

FIG. 10   One of a pair of blue-green and gold sconces, perhaps modeled by Jean-Claude Duplessis. Ca. 1757. 17⅜ in. high. The Metropolitan Museum of Art, New York, Gift of R. Thornton Wilson, 1954, in memory of Florence Ellsworth Wilson.

CHAPTER II

Ornamental Wares

THERE CAN BE NO absolute separation between the useful and the decorative articles of Sèvres, for the reason that the useful is always decorative, and the decorative is so often useful—the flower vases and potpourri vessels, for example. Rather arbitrarily, this section will include only those objects having no immediate function as parts of table services. These ornamental wares might more appropriately be termed presentation pieces, as indeed many of them were conceived as gifts worthy of presentation to persons of high estate.

It is within this category that one becomes aware most readily of the stylistic formula evolved by Sèvres and constituting what virtually amounts to the signature of that factory. The distinguishing features are expressed in the use of colored fields, painted "reserves" and gilding. All these elements may be found in other porcelains, especially Meissen. But in Sèvres there is a greater consistency in organizing the subject matter of the painted ornament; the ground colors are of a more pastel quality, especially during the reign of Louis XV; and the gilding is not only more lavish but is itself embellished with engraved detail.

In ornamental wares the painted reserves are often the outstanding feature. They consist of scenes or other subjects presented within an outlined area of white. Many are true miniature paintings. The picture area may be round, oval, or variously cartouche-shaped. The standard formula for a vase calls for two different kinds of subjects. The front usually exhibits a scene featuring a figure or figures, while the back is differentiated with a floral subject, most often a bouquet. This customary arrangement is very consistent with regard to the obverse, but much more variable on the reverse. Sometimes the floral motif is replaced by a trophy symbolizing love, music, gardening or the like; or, alternatively, by a landscape.

Only rarely does one find any sharp departure from this distinction between front and back. Occasional vases have three figural reserves, or a landscape supplemented by two reserves containing flowers. An apparently unique exception to the rule is a pair of square bulb pots (COLOR PLATE I) on which each of the four sides carries a different type of decorative motif: figural, land-scape, trophy and bouquet. It follows naturally that the gilding assumes four different patterns and that each side should have a ground of a different color: turquoise blue, deep blue, green and rose. This extraordinary pair of vessels, exhibiting the basic repertory of Sèvres decorative schemes, was doubtless intended as an example of virtuosity.

Gold evokes a natural association with a royal product. In the first place, the 1745 franchise of the factory reserved to it the sole right among the makers of French porcelain to use gilding. For this reason it is usually easy to distinguish Vincennes or Sèvres on entering a museum gallery filled with French porcelains. The added sparkle of gold makes an immediate appeal to the eye, and a close inspection, especially of earlier pieces, reveals the lavish thickness of the gold, proclaiming this to be truly a *porcelaine de luxe*. Nor is this all. The

FIG. 11   Vincennes wine glass cooler (*sceau*). Ca. 1750. 4 in. high. The Metropolitan Museum of Art, New York, Gift of Mr. and Mrs. Morris Hawkes, 1924.

gold is tooled with finely engraved lines to produce a pattern of flowers, foliage, spiraled ribbons and various geometric motifs. Even effects of light and shade are produced by burnishing certain details with a polished stone, and leaving others in the mat finish with which the gold emerges from the kiln.

Another area of distinction for Sèvres is the inventiveness of its designers in creating forms new to the field of ceramics. The decorative pieces display this characteristic most effectively. The new shapes vary from simple cylindrical vases (Fig. 11) to incredibly complex vessels like the perforated potpourri jars (Fig. 12).

Especially characteristic was the practice of designing objects to serve a dual purpose. One example is the flower vase with elephant-head handles fitted as candle arms (Fig. 13); another is the gondola-shaped vase (Fig. 15), made to hold aromatic petals or, alternatively, to support flowering narcissus

FIG. 12   Potpourri jar and pair of matching vases in deep blue and green, designed by Duplessis, with bird reserves by François Aloncle. Ca. 1757. Jar 21 in. high; vases 15 in. high. Copyright The Frick Collection, New York.

Opposite above: FIG. 13 Pair of "rose Pompadour" candelabra vases with elephant-head handles; the trunks held candle sockets. Ca. 1756. 15½ in. high. The Metropolitan Museum of Art, New York, Gift of the Samuel H. Kress Foundation, 1958.

Opposite below: FIG. 14 Myrtle-green jardiniere with openwork stand. Date-marked for 1760. 8½ in. high. The Metropolitan Museum of Art, New York, Gift of the Samuel H. Kress Foundation, 1958.

Below: FIG. 15 Gondola-shaped potpourri with blue-green ground. Cupids attributed to Charles-Nicolas Dodin. Date-marked for 1756. 14⅛ × 14½ in. Philadelphia Museum of Art.

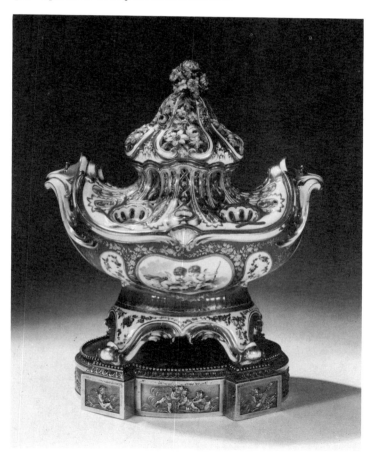

bulbs on its sloping shoulder. Still another type of vase (Fig. 14) is intended
to accommodate cut flowers of different lengths: long ones in its fan-shaped
upper part, and short ones in its perforated stand. Incidentally, the stand
serves as a reservoir to supply water for both sections through the ingenious
device of inserting the pierced stem of the upper portion into the lower.

The same progression from white to colored grounds observed in the useful
wares was shared by the ornamental pieces. Thus the fan-shaped vases of
about 1755–1760 (Fig. 16) and others of the same approximate date were
decorated with charming vignettes, in either blue grisaille or polychrome,
that seemed to float lightly upon the surface of the sparkling white porcelain.
In all too short a time, this whiteness, of a quality unrivaled in French porcelain, was abandoned in favor of colored grounds that provided appropriate
accents to the white, gold and pastel-colored interiors of the time. It may even
be argued that minimizing the use of white detracted from the essential "porcelain quality" of Sèvres, producing an effect of overall color better suited to
objects made of metal, such as copper coated with enamel, for example. It is

Opposite: FIG. 16   Pair of Vincennes jardinieres with openwork stands. Ca. 1755. 7¾ in. high. Walters Art Gallery, Baltimore.

Above: FIG. 17   Pair of deep blue vases with amorous-military subjects attributed to Jean-Louis Morin. Ca. 1765. 16 in. high. The Metropolitan Museum of Art, New York, Gift of the Samuel H. Kress Foundation, 1958.

Right: FIG. 18   Case for dance program (*carnet de bal*) with monogram of Mme du Barry, pale turquoise partridge-eye ground. 1771. 3¼ × 2⅛ in. The Metropolitan Museum of Art, New York, Gift of J. Pierpont Morgan, 1917.

also conceivable that this increased saturation with color tended to encourage a trend in design toward shapes more expressive of the rigidity of metal than of the plasticity of porcelain, as may be seen by comparing Figure 17 and Figure 24.

It was a portentous coincidence that the efflorescence of new forms at Sèvres should have coincided with the period 1756–1763, when Meissen was subjected to the ravages of the Seven Years' War. These were the years in which totally new conceptions such as the gondola vase, the vase *vaisseau à mat* (Fig. 12), the *vase hollandais* (Fig. 14), *vase Hébert* (Fig. 19), *vase à éléphants* (Fig. 13) and others made their appearance. Such extraordinary shapes captured the imagination of Europe and catapulted Sèvres into the front rank of design. The royal porcelain took its place beside French silver, furniture and tapestry, all acknowledged as models for the Western world.

It would be a mistake to assume that progress in design was limited entirely to vase forms. Other types of objects shared in the development. Notable among them were wall sconces boldly concocted of Rococo scrolls (Fig. 10), inkstands like the one belonging to the Electress Elizabeth of Bavaria (Fig. 20) and even souvenirs of the dance (*carnets de bal*) in which ladies kept the names of their partners (Fig. 18). Indeed, the *carnets* were only one among several types of porcelain "toys." Others were buttons, thimbles, cane handles, patch boxes, tobacco or snuff boxes, needle cases, perfume flasks and bonbonnières.

Styles changed with the passage of time, as is strikingly expressed in ornamental pieces. The flamboyance of forms like the *vase à têtes de bouc* (Fig. 21) gave way to the architectural severity of ornamental pieces like the so-called *Fontenoy Vases* at the Metropolitan Museum (Fig. 22). But whereas both types exploited color to enrich their form, a strong trend toward sculptural emphasis asserted itself during the reign of Louis XVI. This is illustrated in the remarkable *vases à jets d'eau* (Fig. 23), and in the advent of porcelain without glaze—a revolutionary innovation of the sculpture studios at Sèvres.

Above: FIG. 19   Deep blue potpourri vase with *vermiculé* gilding, reserve painted by Dodin. Date-marked for 1771. 14⅛ in. high. Alfred de Rothschild Collection, Waddesdon Manor.

Below: FIG. 20   Apple-green inkstand of the Electress Elizabeth of Bavaria. Ca. 1765. 15 in. long. Residenzmuseum., Munich.

Above: FIG. 21 Vase with ram's-head handles. Battle scene, possibly by Morin, framed in *rose marbré* ground. 1758 or 1763. 19 in. high. Henry E. Huntington Library and Art Gallery, San Marino.

Above: FIG. 22 Apple-green turret-vases. Ca. 1758. 22½ in. high. The Metropolitan Museum of Art, New York, Gift of R. Thornton Wilson, 1956, in memory of Florence Ellsworth Wilson.

Above: FIG. 24 Vincennes wall fountain. Ca. 1755. 13¾ in. high. Wadsworth Atheneum, Hartford.

Opposite below: FIG. 23 Pair of fountain vases with dolphin handles, deep blue ground. Ca. 1770–1775. 14⅛ in. high. Walters Art Gallery, Baltimore.

CHAPTER III

Sculptures

THE MANIPULATION OF CLAY into vessels of everyday use has gone hand in hand with the fashioning of figures since prehistoric times. Porcelain clay, late to arrive upon the scene, proved to be no exception. At Sèvres it was employed not only for sculpture in the round, but also for exquisite portrait medallions in low relief.

During the earliest years at Vincennes—the 1740's—single figures and groups were attempted against great technical odds. The clay lacked the tenacity required for small delicate parts and consequently had to be fashioned with thick, heavy walls that tended to develop unsightly fissures during firing. Further, the sheer weight of the clay induced a strong tendency toward sagging and warping in the kiln. These disadvantages can be observed in the *Hercules and Omphale* (Fig. 32).

By 1750, however, the technique and the material had been improved to the point where small figures with delicate details could be fired with a high degree of success. Among the subjects were children adapted from drawings and paintings by François Boucher. Some of these sculptures were made entirely in white; others, like the *Harvester* in Figure 28, were touched with delicate flesh tints or accents of blue in their costumes.

Animal subjects were also attempted. They may have been suggested by those created at Chantilly, where the Duke of Villeroy encouraged his modelers to seek inspiration from the wild and domesticated creatures kept on the grounds of his château. A favorite subject at Vincennes was a *Hound Overcoming a Frenzied Swan* (Fig. 29). This composition is seen variously: in white, entirely covered with gilding or sometimes in bold polychrome. In the entire repertory of Vincennes and Sèvres, however, it is rare to find figures colored in the assertive manner of Meissen. Among the few exceptions are *Girl with a Cage* (Fig. 25), by Blondeau; *Dr. Fagon,* court physician to

FIG. 25 *Girl with a Cage,* Vincennes, by Blondeau (after Boucher). Ca. 1752. Musée National de Céramique, Sèvres.

FIGS. 26 and 27 *Psyche* and *Cupid*, biscuit, on deep blue bases. Model for *Cupid* created by Étienne-Maurice Falconet in 1758, originally commissioned by Mme de Pompadour ca. 1755. Cupid's pose is ambiguous,

indicating Silence (finger to lips) or Mistrust (hand reaching for a quiver).
12 in. high with bases. The Metropolitan Museum of Art, New York,
Bache Collection.

Left: FIG. 28 *Harvester*, Vincennes. Model created by Blondeau in 1752. 7⅞ in. high.

Below: FIG. 29 *Hound Overcoming a Frenzied Swan*, gilded, on contemporary gilt bronze stand. Model created by Blondeau ca. 1752. Group 6⅜ in. high. Walters Art Gallery, Baltimore.

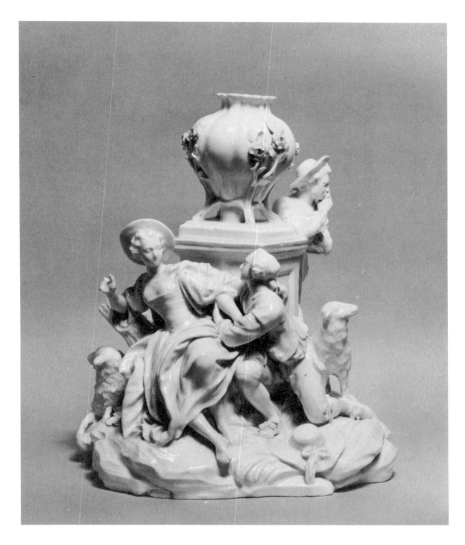

FIG. 30 *Jealousy*, Vincennes. Ca. 1752–1755. 9½ in. high. Wadsworth Atheneum, Hartford.

Above: FIG. 31 *Shepherd and Shepherdess*, Vincennes. Ca. 1750. 8¾ in. high. Museum of Fine Arts, Boston, Forsyth Wickes Collection.

Below: FIG. 32 *Hercules and Omphale*, Vincennes. Ca. 1750. 8¾ in. high. The Metropolitan Museum of Art, New York, Gift of R. Thornton Wilson, 1943, in memory of Florence Ellsworth Wilson.

FIG. 33   *Pygmalion and Galatea*, biscuit. Model created by Falconet in 1763. Group 14½ in. high. Museum of Fine Arts, Boston, Forsyth Wickes Collection.

Louis XIV; and some small figures of birds like those at the Metropolitan Museum of Art and the National Museum of Ceramics at Sèvres.

The most exquisite results were achieved in the modeling of allegorical and thematic subjects, such as river gods, the *Flute Lesson* and *Jealousy* (Fig. 30). These white sculptures are consummate expressions of their medium, conveying much of the idyllic quality and fragility of eighteenth-century society itself.

All of the sculptures discussed above are "typical" porcelain sculptures: they are enveloped in a transparent, colorless glaze that imparts the brilliant sparkle universally associated with porcelain. The type was not to continue unchallenged at Vincennes for very long. About 1750, or shortly thereafter, a revolutionary innovation, that of a glazeless, or biscuit, porcelain was to supersede it and set a new standard for ceramic appreciation. Biscuit porcelain is believed to have been "discovered" by Madame de Pompadour. According to a contemporary account, she became impatient about the progress of some figures she had placed on order and visited the factory to inquire about them. On being told that they were almost ready, lacking only their glaze, she demanded to see them. At first glance she was struck with their resemblance to the color and texture of fine white marble and, accordingly, ordered them to be delivered as they were. With her penchant for setting new fashions, she created an instant demand for biscuit figures.

Just as glazed porcelain arrived on the scene at the psychological moment to be accepted as the ideal medium for expressing the Rococo, so did biscuit appear at the right time to nourish the seeds of the Neoclassical movement that was to become synonymous with the main current of art during the reign of Louis XVI. At Sèvres the leading advocate of the new trend was Étienne-Maurice Falconet, supervisor of the sculpture studios from 1757 until 1766, when he was lured into the employ of Catherine the Great. Most acclaimed among his sculptures in biscuit porcelain were his *Cupid* of 1758 and *Psyche* of about 1762 (Figs. 26 and 27). Within his lifetime and continuing into the present century, these figures have been reproduced in country after country and in a wide variety of media.

Falconet's *Bather* (1758) may well be the earliest manifestation of the Neoclassical style in sculpture. The biscuit porcelain of which it is made is infinitely more appropriate to the dignified treatment of the subject than the more familiar glazed porcelain could have been. Falconet followed the *Bather*

Right: FIG. 34 *The Oracle*, biscuit. Model created by Falconet in 1766. 5½ in. high. The Metropolitan Museum of Art, New York, Gift of R. Thornton Wilson, 1952, in memory of Florence Ellsworth Wilson.

Below: FIG. 35 *The Magic Lantern* or *Curiosity*, biscuit. Model created by Falconet in 1763. 6⅛ × 7 in. The Metropolitan Museum of Art, New York, Bequest of Ella Morris de Peyster, 1958.

with other subjects in the same vein, notably *Pygmalion* of 1763 (Fig. 33) and *Hebe* of 1767. Yet, by a curious inconsistency, he employed the same medium for a series of genre groups depicting children in typically Rococo compositions. Among them are sentimental and moralizing themes in the manner of Boucher or Greuze, observed in such group pieces as *Tourniquet*, *Broken Sabot*, *Schoolmistress* and *Schoolmaster*, which have had a perennially popular appeal.

Falconet was succeeded by Jean-Jacques Bachelier, who looked to the works of other sculptors, both ancient and contemporary, for his designs. Thus in 1768 the *Medici Venus* was reproduced, as were Edme Bouchardon's *Cupid Carving a Bow from the Club of Hercules*, and in 1770, Pigalle's *Venus*, with *Mercury* as a companion figure.

The use of unglazed white porcelain was not limited to sculpture in the round. During the 1750's, a series of fine portraits was launched in the form of bas-relief medallions. Vases in biscuit mark its rarest occurrence (Fig. 36).

Above: FIG. 37 *Parnassus*, biscuit centerpiece sculpted by Louis-Simon Boizot for service of Catherine the Great. It illustrates the inclusion of unglazed sculptures in large services. 1779. 34⅝ in. high. Musée National de Céramique, Sèvres.

Opposite: FIG. 36   Pair of biscuit vases (*vase Fontaine du Barry*) with gilded reliefs. Ca. 1776. 16½ in. high. Museum of Fine Arts, Boston, Gift of Robert Treat Paine.

FIG. 38 *The Three Graces,* one of a pair of biscuit medallions installed on desk of Louis XV to replace the king's monogram. 1794. 6¼ in. high. Château de Versailles.

CHAPTER IV

Porcelain Inlays for Furniture

A VASTLY IMPORTANT but very limited aspect of Sèvres productivity was concerned with the preparation of porcelain plaques to be used as inlays in furniture. Chavagnac and Grollier,[4] referring to developments at Vincennes (and by the same token implying a date not later than 1756), specifically mention a project in which sixteen plaques were copied from Chinese enamel originals in the collection of Machault. These plaques were described as having been mounted by "BURB" in two pieces of furniture having a ground of blue lacquer. Thus we have evidence that among the earliest users of such plaques was one of the most eminent cabinetmakers of Paris, Bernard II Vanrisamburgh, whose stamp bearing his abbreviated name appears on some of the world's costliest furniture.

This specialized use of porcelain was immediately taken over by a group of privileged art purveyors, the *marchands-merciers*, or "decorators" of Paris, who maintained shops where fine furniture and other objects of luxury were sold to the wealthiest patrons of the day. These merchants acted as intermediaries between the furniture makers and the Sèvres factory on the one hand and apparently as designers or advisers to their clients on the other. In this way they exercised a monopoly on the market for ornamental plaques and became the pace-setters for a new category of furniture that was costly in the extreme. Porcelain, in the hands of these *marchands-merciers*, became not merely an adjunct but an equal partner of the fashionable exotic woods and costly mounts of sculptured gilt bronze that went into this exclusive kind of furniture.

Much skill and planning were required to prepare these plaques in the correct sizes and shapes to fit into surfaces of the furniture with the precision of pieces in a jigsaw puzzle. Not the least factor was the shrinkage to which all

---

4. Count X. de Chavagnac and Marquis de Grollier, *Histoire des Manufactures Françaises de Porcelaine*, Paris, 1906, p. 143. It is to be noted that Vienna, not Vincennes, was the first European factory to make plaques of porcelain for this purpose. Many were installed about 1724 in a room at the Dubsky Palace, which has since been removed from its site near Brünn to the Museum für Angewändte Kunst, Vienna. Even earlier, panels of Delft faience, and of course, Chinese porcelain, were used in this way.

Above: FIG. 39 Pair of plaques from a set of mosaic panels used on low cabinet. Left: painted by Noël. Right: painted by Cornailles. Date-marked for 1764. 4 in. square. The Metropolitan Museum of Art, New York, Gift of the Samuel H. Kress Foundation, 1958.

Left: FIG. 40 Plaque, painted by Bulidon, from the side of an upright secretary. Date-marked for 1773. 12½ × 8 in. The Metropolitan Museum of Art, New York, Gift of the Samuel H. Kress Foundation, 1958.

FIG. 41   Lady's writing desk with seventeen plaques attributed to Denis Levé and Pierre *jeune*. Date-marked for 1768. The Metropolitan Museum of Art, New York, Gift of the Samuel H. Kress Foundation, 1958.

Above: FIG. 42   *Bureau du Roi* of Louis XV showing installation of biscuit plaque in Figure 38. Château de Versailles.

Opposite: FIG. 43   Upright secretary inset with Sèvres porcelain plaque and Wedgwood jasperware medallions, the plaque with the mark of Bouillat *père*. Ca. 1790. Plaque 16 × 13½ in. The Metropolitan Museum of Art, New York, Gift of the Samuel H. Kress Foundation, 1958.

porcelain is subject when fired. Therefore the scale of each piece as it was fashioned had to be increased by a calculated percentage. Unlike dinner plates, in which the warpage could be kept to a minimum (possibly as a result of a process called jiggering, by which they were formed), the production of plaques was fraught with extraordinary difficulties in terms of warpage and cracks produced by uneven shrinkage. Some idea of the severity of this problem may be gained from a report made in 1796,[5] which stated that only one out of every five plaques survived the initial firing.

5. Emile Molinier, *Histoire Générale des Arts Appliqués à l'Industrie du Ve à la Fin du XVIIIe Siècle*, Vol. III: *Le Mobilier au XVIIIe Siècle*, Paris: E. Lévy, 1898, pp. 181, 182.

53

COLOR PLATE II: Hard-paste dessert plate executed by Jean-Jacques Dieu in imitation of Chinese lacquer, details in platinum. Date-marked for 1792. 9½ in. The Metropolitan Museum of Art, New York, Gift of Lewis Einstein, 1962.

Right: FIG. 44 Plaque from a wall barometer painted by Dodin. Open page records the transit of Venus in June 1769. Date-marked for 1769. 5¼ × 4¾ in. The Metropolitan Museum of Art, New York, Gift of the Samuel H. Kress Foundation, 1958.

Below: FIG. 45 Plaque from a marriage coffer, probably painted by Pierre *jeune*. Deep green and gilded border. 1768–1770. 5⅜ × 8⅛ in. The Metropolitan Museum of Art, New York, Gift of the Samuel H. Kress Foundation, 1958.

FIG. 46   Clock of gilt bronze inlaid with Sèvres. Ca. 1770. 23⅝ in. high. The
Metropolitan Museum of Art, New York, Gift of the Samuel H. Kress Foundation, 1958.

During the period of the Rococo, lozenge-shaped panels with wavy edges were at times set in diagonal trellis patterns on the fronts of commodes (Fig. 39). Later, under Neoclassical influences, plaques assumed a larger size and more regular shapes (round or oblong), which were conducive to their installation in horizontal rows. Small ones were used to panel the flat surfaces of ladies' writing desks (Fig. 41) and tables; large ones decorated the fronts of *secrétaires* (Fig. 40). A notable exception to this general rule is the *secrétaire* in Figure 43, in which medallions of Wedgwood jasperware supplement the single large floral panel of Sèvres.

A second class of furniture inlay consists of unglazed plaques resembling Wedgwood and featuring classical subjects in white relief upon a blue ground. While they sometimes lack the crispness and contrast of English jasperware, they nevertheless serve to strike a similar ceramic note in furniture of a pronounced Neoclassical flavor. One notable installation is the ebony and ormolu commode of severe architectural simplicity, now in the Hermitage, Leningrad. Another is the medallion *The Three Graces* (Fig. 38) that was installed in the famous desk of Louis XV as a replacement for the king's monogram in marquetry, which was looked upon as a feudalistic symbol in the days of the Revolution.

To return to the painted plaque, it is especially intriguing to conjure up the image of a coach set with these precious panels. Just such a creation, belonging to a courtesan called La Beaupré, is reported by Louis Petit de Bachaumont (d. 1771) in his *Mémoires secrets*; he saw it at Longchamps in 1764, in all its glory.

FIG. 47   Plaque with deep green and gilded border from a low cabinet. Ca. 1770. 2¼ × 11⅝ in. The Metropolitan Museum of Art, New York, Gift of the Samuel H. Kress Foundation, 1958.

CHAPTER V

Flowers

ANY SUMMARY OF Sèvres' artistic production would be incomplete if it did not take into account the truly important role of the most delicate and certainly the most numerous item turned out in the early years: flowers. Assembled and tinted petal by petal, then fitted to stems of wire, they were available either as single blossoms or as nosegays. One use to which they were put was the embellishment of vases, particularly vases of the shape called Medici. By means of slip (a watery solution of clay), small clusters of blossoms were attached to the sides. Useless as handles because of their fragility, they nevertheless served to soften the contours and reduce the solidity of these rather massive vessels. Similarly, they were used to ornament *pots pourris*, candlesticks and sconces—as in the pair of three-branched wall lights owned by the Dauphine Marie Josèphe at Versailles, which were garnished with more than a dozen varieties of porcelain flowers. The most characteristic application of all, however, was the use of a flower as the knob or finial for the covers of dishes to be used at table. A carnation became the virtual signature of Vincennes-Sèvres manufacture.

In the eighteenth century, as today, artificial flowers were used to fill vases when live blooms were not readily available. A colorful legend supports this claim. It concerns Madame de Pompadour during the early days when the Vincennes enterprise was struggling against financial odds. According to the story, the marquise, scheming to gain the support of the king for this venture, arranged to have the conservatory at her new Château de Bellevue lavishly stocked with Vincennes vases, each filled with a profusion of colorful porcelain flowers scented with the finest perfumes. One cold, snowy night, she ushered Louis into this heady environment. The impact was electric, and the outcome was as anticipated.

Plans were soon under way to reserve a one-third interest for the king in the

FIG. 48   Vincennes vase with about seventy flowers and two figure groups, on gilt bronze mount. 1749. Overall height 45¼ in. The Zwinger, Dresden.

FIG. 49   Nosegays of Vincennes flowers mounted on painted wire stems. Ca. 1750.
Musée National de Céramique, Sèvres.

new organization, and to move the factory to a more adequate site at Sèvres, conveniently near the new residence of La Pompadour. Her influence upon the furtherance of the manufactory and its standards proved to be incalculable, but may be summed up in a material way by stating that three years after its transfer to Sèvres the factory became fully the property of the king, a possession that was jealously prized by him and also by his successor, who stood by it stoutly during the desperate days of the Revolution.

So great was the skill of the Vincennes flowermakers that as early as 1748 the Duc de Luynes wrote, "This manufactuary is now superior to that of Saxony for the making of flowers."[6] It was in the same year that the Dauphine Marie Josèphe, granddaughter of Augustus the Strong, sent her father the magnificent white vase filled with tinted porcelain flowers that is still to be found at the Zwinger in Dresden. It is flanked by two beautifully modeled white figures and enhanced with an exquisite plinth of gilt bronze (Fig. 48). A corresponding ensemble, sold to Queen Marie Leczinska, cost 2,600 livres.

Surely, then, flowers must have been a favorable factor in attracting financial support to the manufactory. In 1745 the organization had been thoroughly restructured. The interest of Madame de Pompadour and the king helped to attract a brilliant array of talent. Every branch of the operation was affected. The administration gained by the appointment of Boileau as general manager. Technical aspects were placed under the supervision of Hellot (1685–1766), and Pierre-Joseph Macquer (1718–1784), celebrated chemists and members of the Academy of Sciences. The artistic staff was improved by the appointment of Bachelier as supervisor, with Falconet in 1757 in charge of the sculptural branch. The skill and collaboration of these well-qualified specialists opened the most glamorous chapter in the history of Sèvres, a phase that survived until the fall of Louis XVI in the early 1790's.

---

6. In his *Mémoires*, under the date of April 13, 1748, as quoted by Auscher, *op. cit.*, p. 43.

FIG. 50 *Table of the Marshals*, top inlaid with fourteen portrait medallions of Napoleon and his favorite officers. Painted by Jean-Baptiste Isabey. 1806–1810. 38¼ in. Château de Malmaison.

CHAPTER VI

Sèvres Since the Revolution

FROM THE TIME of the Revolution until the present, the Sèvres factory has remained out of private hands, though protected alternately by a republican government or the reigning monarch. Although the organization has seen many changes during this time, the established practice of making generous gifts to prominent persons, especially the heads of foreign states, was never discontinued. Thus the role of the factory as an instrument for state propaganda remained unchanged. Soon after the factory was nationalized in 1792, Napoleon was one of the first to recognize the advantages of preserving Sèvres and other former royal workshops, such as Beauvais, the Gobelins and Savonnerie. While First Consul, he ordered a tall vase in *beau bleu*, with gilt bronze mounts by Pierre-Philippe Thomire. Valued at 50,000 francs, it was given by him to the "Count of Livourne, King of Etruria." Another of his gifts was a pair of great porcelain candelabra, also mounted in bronze by Thomire; the recipient was Pope Pius VII.

As emperor, Napoleon again showed his personal interest by transferring the factory from the jurisdiction of the Bureau of Arts and Manufactures to the Intendance Générale de la Maison de l'Empereur. This act brought the assurance of a regular budget, although the emperor also contributed from his own pocket from time to time, as had Louis XV and Louis XVI. The imperial palaces were refurbished with the greatest variety of porcelains: from columns to clocks, vases to busts, and tables to candelabra. The famous *Table of the Marshals*, now at Malmaison, is an impressive example (Fig. 50). Ordered in 1806, it memorialized the emperor and his chief officers in portrait plaques painted by Isabey and set as a mosaic to form the top. Talleyrand, as minister of state, wooed Russia by presenting Czar Alexander in 1807 and 1808 with two great services, the *Olympic* and the *Egyptian*, the latter decorated with scenes of Napoleon's campaign in Egypt. Indeed, so great was the emperor's interest in Sèvres that he visited the studios at least once a year to choose presents of state. This practice had much the same effect upon the economy of the factory as had the former Christmas exhibitions of Louis XV at Versailles and Louis XVI there and at the Louvre: it cast the monarch in the role of principal salesman.

Internally, the organization was improved by the brilliant administration of Alexandre Brongniart, who brought the technical training of an engineer and mineralogist to his task. One of his first acts, in 1800, was to sell the factory's outmoded stocks of porcelain in order to reduce the operating deficit. A more lasting contribution was his invention of an improved hard paste consisting of kaolin, feldspar, quartz and chalk.[7] This was a high-firing, tough material, especially well suited to the requirements of tablewares. Under Brongniart's leadership, the quality of work turned out by the artists also rose to new heights.

The prevailing style, Empire, was as fittingly named for Napoleon's reign as was the politically generated style of Louis XIV. Vases and certain table porcelains assumed forms borrowed from Etruscan vases, of which the factory owned a collection. The result was that ovoid and cylindrical shapes soon became dominant. For decoration, themes as diversified as Egyptian landscapes, mythological scenes, cameo effects and illustrations of La Fontaine's *Fables* were employed. The use of gold became blatantly ostentatious. It was no longer reserved for borders alone; cups and occasionally other vessels were often entirely coated inside with gilding. A new green, made from chromium, was introduced in 1802.[8] It and a deep blue (*beau bleu*) surviving from the eighteenth century became the predominant ground colors of the period. Transfer-printing of designs from paper (decalcomania) also began early in the century, as evidenced by a plate decorated in this technique given to Napoleon in 1808 by General Savary.[9]

The renaissance of Sèvres under Napoleon quite naturally suffered a reversal after Waterloo. The year 1815 brought the Allied occupation, during which Prussian troops were housed and fed in the capacious building where the world's most prestigious porcelain had been made. A tribute of 10,000 francs was levied against the organization, and porcelains of enormous value were seized. The victors claimed "everything relative to the Bonaparte family," of which the porcelains alone were estimated to be worth 53,000 francs.

7. A. Brongniart, *Traité des Arts Céramiques ou des Poteries*, Vol. II, Paris: Béchet Jeune, 1854, pp. 17 *et seq.*

8. Pierre Verlet and Serge Grandjean, *Sèvres*, Paris: Gérard le Prat, 1953, p. 64.

9. *Ibid.*

The long period between the Restoration and the end of the Second Empire (1814–1870) was not particularly distinguished for artistic or administrative progress, although technical improvements continued to be made. One concerned the process called *coulage*, which about 1814 was taken over from the Paris factories, where it had been in use for a couple of decades. This method was based essentially on flowing the liquid paste upon flat slabs of plaster. Many of the plaques were inset into cigar boxes and *guéridon* tables, although with the increase in size that Brongniart's refinements made possible, they also found a market as panels for paintings. Ever larger sizes were attempted, and by the 1830's panels about four feet long and two and a half wide—adequate for sizable paintings—were achieved. Brongniart describes the process in detail in his *Traité des Arts Céramiques ou des Poteries* (Vol. I, pp. 147–155).

Among three-dimensional pieces there was a renewed demand for reticulated designs—that is, those made of openwork, like a stencil. In a sense this was a return to an eighteenth-century practice, except for the important difference that in earlier times the pierced openings served the useful purpose of accommodating flower stems or bulbs. In the new usage the pierced walls were purely ornamental, even to the point of making an object quite useless except as an ornament (for example, of a goblet with a pierced bowl).

During the second quarter of the century, a period roughly equivalent to the reign of Louis Philippe, an attempt was made to revive the prestige of biscuit. In part it took its cue from the development of the plaque, and aimed for impressive size to attract attention. A monumental vase, the *Phidias* vase, more than six feet high, was fashioned, but it failed to stir much interest in the material. Portrait busts of about life size were also turned out at this time. Those made from 1863 onward carried as a mark the crossed *L* cipher, impressed into the paste and left uncolored. (See Appendix for information on marks.)

By mid-century, Sèvres had yielded to the popular eclecticism in style, a taste not greatly admired today. The printing press had placed into the hands of designers a flood of ideas too voluminous for most to cope with judiciously. They reacted by borrowing without inhibition, creating novel interpretations calculated to stun the beholder with their opulence. Not a square inch that could be ornamented was left free to fight for its life in this era when artists, like nature, abhorred a vacuum.

The degeneration of esthetic standards became so marked that a Commission de Perfectionnement was formed to stem the decline. Shortly after 1870 it issued a report containing this statement: "The feeling for decoration is often weak, but what is apparent above all is the absence of principles of art, and evidence of appropriate training."

Strenuous efforts were made to recapture the position of artistic leadership. In the tradition of 1745, major artists were called upon to work in concert for the advancement of the cause. The sculptor Carrier-Belleuse, appointed director of art in 1876, secured the collaboration of such sculptors as Rodin, Rude and Dalou, and that of the painter Chéret as well. Improvement came, but only gradually. The flowing forms and electric colors of Art Nouveau gave a needed coherence to the style, as became evident in the Sèvres exhibition at the Paris Exposition of 1900.

From that time until the present, Sèvres has held an esteemed position in the ceramic world. Its products, always fine in quality, have maintained their individuality throughout a succession of influences from Japan, Scandinavia and elsewhere. Today they remain French, with all the freshness and vivacity that that implies. Yet on the shelves of the showroom at Sèvres, scattered among the smartest examples of the newest modes, are table porcelains that Louis Quinze and Louis Seize could have lived with very comfortably.

FIG. 51   Spyglass with bronze fittings. Ca. 1765. 2¼ in. long, 1 in. diameter. Mr. and Mrs. Charles B. Wrightsman Collection, New York.

I

The marks and dates appearing here have been gathered from several standard sources. The writer particularly wishes to thank Mlle Marcelle Brunet for her generosity in permitting him to use the material found in her invaluable book.

CHAVAGNAC, COUNT X. DE and GROLLIER, MARQUIS DE. *Histoire des Manufactures Françaises de Porcelaine.* Paris, 1906.

LECHEVALLIER-CHEVIGNARD, G. *La Manufacture de Porcelaine de Sèvres.* Paris, 1908.

HONEY, W. B. *European Ceramic Art.* London, 1953.

BRUNET, MARCELLE. *Les Marques de Sèvres.* Paris, 1953.

ERIKSEN, SVEND. *Sèvres Porcelain: The Alfred de Rothschild Collection at Waddesdon Manor.* London, 1968.

I. Factory and Date Marks in Color—On Glazed Porcelain Only

It is not known with certainty how the earliest Vincennes porcelain was marked, if indeed it was marked at all. However, enough has survived from the late forties and early fifties, as judged on stylistic grounds, to establish that the royal cipher was used with reasonable consistency during that period. This mark consisted of two *L*'s (for Louis) interlaced to form a monogram. It was painted in blue over the glaze, with which it became amalgamated in the process of firing. The letters, painted with a brush, were often quite simple, but at times were embellished with dots and flourishes of various kinds, as illustrated below. In the nineteenth century, printed factory marks are characteristic.

REIGNS OF LOUIS XV AND XVI (until 1793)

These marks are usually in blue, but may be in other colors.

 The royal cipher, sometimes embellished with flourishes. Used at Vincennes from about 1740–1752, when only soft-paste porcelain was made.

Cipher with date letters A through D, used 1753–1756 at Vincennes. With sub-sequent letters, used at Sèvres until 1793. Reserved for soft paste.

 Crowned cipher of Sèvres, used about 1768–1770 until 1793. Reserved for hard paste.

Date letters were used with the above marks. Beginning in 1753 and lasting until 1793, the factory mark was modified to include a coded date, represented by a letter or pair of letters, as shown in the chart below. These letters may be either capital or small, and may be placed either within the *L*'s or outside.

A (Vincennes).... 1753	P 1768	EE 1782
B „ 1754	Q 1769	FF 1783
C „ 1755	R 1770	GG 1784
D 1756	S 1771	HH 1785
E 1757	T 1772	II 1786
F 1758	U 1773	JJ 1787
G 1759	V 1774	KK 1788
H 1760	X 1775	LL 1789
I 1761	Y 1776	MM 1790
J 1762	Z 1777	NN 1791
K 1763		OO 1792
L 1764	AA 1778	PP 1793
M 1765	BB 1779	QQ 1794
N 1766	CC 1780	RR 1795
O 1767	DD 1781	

PP is frequently seen; QQ and RR are not unknown, but may be regarded as unauthorized holdovers into the time of the First Republic.

FIRST REPUBLIC 1793–1804

Marks in blue 1793–1800   Mark in color, usually blue, or gilding
                                                           1800–1802

R *R.F* R.F   *Sèvres*
Sèvres *Sèvres* *Sèvres*

Mark in red 1803–May, 1804

FIRST EMPIRE 1804–1815

Mark in red 1804–1809
(with date marks)

Mark in red 1810–1814
(with date marks)

*Date marks
beginning with the year IX of the
Revolutionary Calendar, 1801

T9 . . . IX, 1801	9 1809
X . . . . X, 1802	10 1810
II . . . XI, 1803	oz 1811
⹀ . . . XII, 1804	dz 1812
-‖- . . XIII, 1805	tz 1813
⏝ . . XIV, 1806	qz 1814
7 1807	qn 1815
8 1808	sz 1816

*These marks are frequently used in conjunction with
factory marks of 1801–1816*

REIGN OF LOUIS XVIII 1814–1824

Mark in blue, usually with abbreviated dates

REIGN OF CHARLES X 1824–1830

Marks in blue with abbreviated dates
1824–1828

Marks in blue with abbreviated dates
1829–1830

REIGN OF LOUIS PHILIPPE 1830–1848

Mark in blue with abbreviated date for 1830

Mark in chrome green with abbreviated dates 1845–1848

Mark in blue or gold with abbreviated dates 1831–1834

Mark in gold or blue 1845–1848

Mark in blue or gold 1834–1845

Mark in blue or gold 1848

Mark in blue or gold 1848

SECOND REPUBLIC 1848–1852

Mark in chrome green with abbreviated dates

Marks in red with abbreviated dates

SECOND EMPIRE 1852–1870

Mark in chrome green for hard paste with abbreviated dates

Mark in red with abbreviated dates 1852–1854

Marks for hard paste with abbreviated date
1854

Marks for soft paste with abbreviated date
1854

Marks in red with abbreviated dates
1855–1870

THIRD REPUBLIC 1871–1940

Mark with abbreviated date 1871–1899
Color identifies type of paste: chrome green
for hard paste; deep blue for new formula
hard paste, 1882–1899; light blue, old formula, revived, soft paste; black, new formula
soft paste.

Mark in red with abbreviated dates
1872–1899

Mark in red with abbreviated date
1871

Mark in underglaze brown, also impressed or
in relief, used on porcelaneous stoneware
1888–1891

II. Workers' Marks

Another practice begun in 1753 was that of adding to the mark various letters or symbols to identify the painters or gilders who shared in decorating a given piece. They are usually painted in blue, but are seen occasionally in other colors. The mark of the gilder Vincent is consistently done in gold. Very infrequently, the marks of other gilders, date letters and even factory marks are found in gold.

In addition to the painted marks of the decorators, Sèvres was frequently inscribed with a variety of marks incised into the paste while it was still damp. These marks, dealing in one way or another with the processing of the porcelain, may be letters, numerals, symbols or a combination of these elements. In 1967 and 1968 the writer investigated the meaning of these marks with the aid of a computer. He succeeded in identifying certain of the alphabetical marks with the names of potters who were known to be in the employ of Sèvres at the time indicated by the date marks on the porcelains. These identifications were confirmed by comparing the handwriting of the marks with the signatures on the factory payroll, where each worker was required to sign opposite his name upon receiving his wages. And since the payroll listed each employee according to his occupation, it became possible to determine the nature of the work done by each signer. The following are a few sample marks, along with the names and occupations uncovered in this way: "da" stands for Danet, a turner; "C.N." identifies the sculptor Chanou; and "Bo" represents Bono, a *répareur*. These findings indicate that at least three types of workers were responsible for the incised letters that are so often found on the underside of Sèvres ornaments and tablewares. It is reasonable to expect that by this process more than names and occupations may be brought out of obscurity. By correlating the incised marks with observable data (such as type of object, ground color, principal motifs, nature of the paste, etc.) and adding the information that can readily be deciphered from the painted marks (the dates, names of painters and gilders), the computer should provide some insight into areas of which we are now almost totally ignorant. For example, we may learn how large orders were processed, how many types of objects were fashioned by a single individual, the periods during which certain types of objects were in greatest demand and the pattern in which hard paste superseded soft paste. There is one other intriguing possibility: the findings of the computer should reveal instances in which marks and dates, for example, are seriously out of agreement. To do so would be to wave a warning flag against forgeries. This service in itself would be a valuable aid, as Sèvres has suffered more from tampering and outright faking than any other porcelain.

Explanation of the tables of marks

There are two basic divisions in the marks:

1. Factory marks and related date marks (pp. 65–69). They are arranged chronologically under historical periods, and are either painted or printed upon the porcelains.

2. Workers' marks, representing two broad categories in one list:

A. Painters and gilders. The marks are usually painted in blue, although gold and other colors are sometimes used.

B. Sculptors and potters (identified by asterisks). The marks are incised into the porcelain and are uncolored.

Where possible, workers' marks are arranged alphabetically, their position governed by the following rules:

Single letters in order of complexity, with upper case preceding lower case, and Roman preceding script; *two or more letters*, separate followed by conjoined. If the leading letter is reversed, it is read as if normally placed; *monograms* of three or four initials are listed in a separate category; so are the *non-alphabetic marks*, chiefly numerals and symbols.

A worker may have more than one listing if he has two or more marks that do not fall into alphabetical sequence.

Names written in full do not appear in this compilation.

In interpreting the workers' marks it is important to correlate them with the appropriate factory marks and date marks.

A — AUVILLAIN*
1877–after 1900

A A — ASSELIN, Charles-Éloi
1765–1804

A.

A — LAPIERRE, Auguste*
1833–1843

A — RICHARD, Auguste
1811–1848

A — ARCHELAIS, Jules
1865–1902

AB — BLANCHARD, Alexandre
1878–1901

A.B. — BRACHARD jeune, Alexandre*
1784–1792, 1795–1799,
1802–1827

AB — BARRÉ, Louis-Désiré
1846–1881

AB — BONNUIT, Achille-Louis
1858–1862, 1865–1894

AB — BOULLEMIER, Antoine-Gabriel
1802–1842

B — BELET, Adolphe
1881–1882

AB — BRIFFAUT, Alphonse-
Théodore-Jean*
1848–1890

A.C. — CIEUTAT, Alphonse*
1894–1928

A — COURSAGET
1881–1886

AD — DAVID, François-Alexandre
1844–1881

AD — DUMAIN, Alphonse*
1884–1928

A.D — DUCLUZEAU, Mme Marie-
Adélaïde
1818–1848

AD — DAMMOUSE, Pierre-Adolphe*
1852–1880

AD — DAVID, François-Alexandre
1844–1881

AD — DUBOIS, Alexandre*
1896–1915

AF — FOURNIER, Anatole
1878–1926

AL — LIGUÉ, Denis
1881–1911

ALA —

Ael — ALLARD, Jean-Baptiste*
1832–1841

A — LACOUR, Armand*
1895–1911

A — LONGUET, Alexandre*
1840–1876

AM — MEYER, Alfred
1858–1871

AM — MORIOT, François-Adolphe
1843–1844

ap — PERCHERON, Alexandre*
1827–1864

AR — POUPART, Antoine-Achille
1815–1848

R APOIL, Charles-Alexis
    1851–1864

B BELET, Émile
    1876–1900

B BOUVRAIN, Antoine-Louis
    1826–1848

O BOULANGER père
    1754–1784

B. BARRÉ
    1773–1774, 1776–1778

B BALDISSERONI, Shiridani
    1860–1879

B BARRAT l'oncle
    1769–1791

B. BRACHARD aîné, Jean-Charles-
    Nicolas*
    1782–1824, or one of the
    BOUGONS working between
    1754 and 1812

B.T BOITEL, Charles-Marie-Pierre
    1797–1822

BD BAUDOUIN père
    1750–1800

BD

Bf BOULLEMIER fils, Hilaire-
    François
    1817–1855

BG BÉRANGER, Antoine
    1807–1846

Bh BOULLEMIER fils, Hilaire-
    François
    1817–1855

Bn BULIDON
    1763–1792

Bo BONO, Étienne-Henri*
    1754–1781

Bt BOQUET, Louis-Honoré*
    1815–1860

Bx BUTEUX, Théodore
    1786–1822

By. BAILLY père
    1753–1767

Bv BOURDOIS*
    1773–1774

C COUTURIER, Claude
    1762–1775

C. CASTEL
    1772–1797

B BARRIAT, Charles
    1848–1883

C.C. CONSTANS, Charles-Louis
    1803–1840

CC CABAU, Eugène-Charles
    1847–1885

C.T. CONSTANTIN, Abraham
    1813–1848

CD DEVELLY, Jean-Charles
    1813–1848

C.D. DESNOYERS-CHAPPONET aîné
    1788–1804, 1810–1828

ch. CHABRY fils, Étienne-Jean
    1765–1787

C.L ch.L — LUCAS, Charles
1878–1910

C L — DELAHAYE, Charles-François-Jules*
1818–1852

cm cm — COMMELIN, Michel-Gabriel
1768–1802

Cn — CHANOU jeune, Henri-Florentin*
1746–1779, 1785

C.P — CAPRONNIER, François
1812–1819

cp — CHAPPUIS aîné, Antoine-Joseph*
1761–1787

CR — ROBERT, Charles*
1889–1930

CV — VILLION, Charles*
1894–1941

D — DORÉ, Pierre
1829–1865

D — DELATRE cadet*
1754–1758

D D.. — DUSOLLE
1768–1774

D.. —

D. — TARDY, Claude-Antoine
1755–1795

da — DANET père*
1759–after 1780

DE — DROUET, Ernest-Émile
1878–1920

DF — DELAFOSSE, Denis
1804–1815

D.F. — DAVIGNON, Jean-François
1807–1815

DG — DERICHWEILER, Jean-Charles-Gérard
1855–1884

D.C — DROUET, Gilbert
1785–1825

D.G. — GODIN, Mme Catherine
1806–1828

Dh — DEUTSCH
1803–1819

D.I — DIDIER père 1787–1825, or fils, Charles-Antoine
1819–1848

D D D — DEVICQ, Jules*
1881–1928

D.VB — BOULLEMIER, Mlle Virginie
1814–1842

D.P. — DEPÉRAIS, Claude-Antoine
1794–1822

DR — DRAND 1764–1775, 1780

DT — DUTANDA, DUTENDA, Nicolas
1765–1802

D — DOAT, Taxile
1879–1905

D.y — DUROSEY, Charles-Christian-Marie
1802–1830

E — LATACHE, Étienne
1867–1879

Mark	Entry
ℰ.	OUINT, Édouard* 1888–1893
E·R	APOIL, Mme Suzanne-Estelle 1865–1892
ℬ	BULOT, Eugène-Alexandre 1855–1883
E.D.	DROUET, Ernest-Émile 1878–1920
ℰ de ℳ	MAUSSION, Mlle de 1862–1870
Ж	ESCALLIER, Mme Éléonore 1874–1888
EF	FROMANT, Eugène 1855–1885
℈	GUILLEMAIN, Ambroise- Ernest-Louis 1864–1885
ℋ	HALLION, Eugène 1870, 1872–1874, 1876–1893
EL	LEROY, Eugène-Éléonor 1855–1891
ℳ	MORIOT, Mlle Élise 1881–1886
ℙ	PORCHON 1880–1884
ER	RICHARD, Eugène 1833–1872
ℜ	RÉJOUX, Émile-Bernard 1858–1893
ℰ.𝒮	SIMARD, Eugène 1880–1908

Mark	Entry
ℰ·3.	HUMBERT, Jules-Eugène 1851–1870
F	FALCONET, Étienne-Maurice* 1757–1766
F	FALLOT 1773–1790
ℾ	FERNEX, Jean-Baptiste de* ca. 1756
ℱ	FONTAINE, Jean-Joseph 1825–1857
f	LEVÉ, Félix 1777–1779
f 𝒮	PFEIFFER 1771–1800
ℱ.ℬ	BOULLEMIER, François- Antoine 1806–1838
ℬ	BARBIN, François-Hubert 1815–1849
F C	COURCY, Alexandre-Frédéric de 1865–1886
ℱ.C.	CHARRIN, Mlle Fanny 1814–1826
ℱ	FICQUENET, Charles 1864–1881
ℱ ℱ	FISCHBAG, Charles* 1834–1850
ℱ.G.	GOUPIL, Frédéric 1859–1878
F.𝒮	

Mark	Name
ℋ	HALLION, François 1865–1895
ℱM	MÉRIGOT, Maximilien-Ferdinand 1845–1872, 1879–1884
ℙ	PAILLET, Fernand 1879–1888, 1893
ℛ	RÉGNIER, Joseph-Ferdinand* 1826–1830, 1836–1870
ɣᵉ	VAUBERTRAND, François 1822–1848
ƒx ƒi	FUMEZ 1777–1804
G	GENEST, Jean-Baptiste-Étienne 1752–1789
𝒢...	GODIN, François-Aimé* 1813–1848
𝒢ℬ	BOTEREL, Georges* 1888–1933
𝒢𝒟	DERICHWEILLER, Jean-Charles-Gérard 1855–1884
𝑔𝑑. 𝒢𝒥.	GÉRARD, Claude-Charles 1771–1824
𝑔.𝑔.	GEORGET, Jean 1801–1823
GL	LEBARQUE, Georges* 1895–1916
⊈	GÉBLEUX, Léonard 1883–1928
𝒢ᵈ.ℛ	GOBERT, Alfred-Thompson 1849–1891
ÇR	ROBERT, Mme Louise 1835–1840
𝒢t	GRÉMONT jeune 1769–1775, 1778–1781
𝒢u	GANEAU, Pierre-Louis 1813–1831
ⱱ 𝒳	VIGNOL, Gustave 1881–1909
H	HOURY, Pierre 1752–1755
ƅ	LAROCHE, de 1759–1802
ℎc.	HÉRICOURT ca. 1755
⧻C ℛ	RENARD, Henri ca. 1881
ℎ.𝒟.	HUARD, Pierre 1811–1846
ℎℯ.	HÉRICOURT jeune 1770–1773, 1776–1777
HF	FARAGUET, Mme 1857–1879
ℍ ℍ.	LASSERRE, Henri* 1886–1931
HP.	PRÉVOST aîné 1754–1793, or le second 1757–1797
HR	ROBERT, Henri* 1889–1933
HS	SILL 1881–1887
⊦	TRAGER, Henri 1887–1909

HU   UHLRICH, Henri
     1879–1925

ły   HUNY (doubtful mark)
     1785–1800, 1810

IC   CHANOU, Jean-Baptiste*
     1779–1825

J. J   JUBIN 1772–1775

J.A   ANDRÉ, Jules
     1840–1869

J ᵃ   JACOB-BER, Moïse
     1814–1848

A   ARCHELAIS, Jules
     1865–1902

JB   BOILEAU fils aîné*
     1773–1781

J.C   CÉLOS, Jules-François
     1865–1895

J.C.   TRAGER, Jules
     1847, 1854–1873

JC.   CHAPPUIS jeune
     1772–1777

JD.   CHANOU, Mme mère
     1779–1800

E.E   JARDEL, Bernard-Louis-Émile
     1886–1913

E E   JULIENNE, Alexis-Étienne
     1837–1849

R Jh. R   Jh.R   RICHARD, Nicolas-Joseph
     1833–1872

j ħ.   HENRION aîné
     1770–1784

JL   LAMBERT, Henri-Lucien
     1859–1899

JR   RÉGNIER, Hyacinthe*
     1825–1863

J.   LEGAY, Jules-Eugène*
     1861–1895

JL   LIANCE fils aîné*
     1769–1810

J.G   GÉLY, Léopold-Jules-Joseph*
     1851–1889

J.n.   CHAUVEAUX fils
     1773–1783

JQ   JAQUOTOT or JACQUOTOT,
     Mme Marie-Victoire
     1801–1842

JR   RISBOURG, Julien*
     1895–1925

JR   ROGER, Thomas-Jules*
     1852–1886

jt   THÉVENET fils
     1752–1758

KK...   DODIN, Charles-Nicolas
     1754–1802

L   LE CAT*
     1872–after 1900

L   LEVÉ, Denis
     1754–1805

L   LECLERC, Auguste*
     1897–1911

L.   COUTURIER,
     entered 1783

B BLANCHARD, Louis-Étienne-Frédéric
1848–1880

B BELET, Louis
1878–1913

LB LE BEL jeune
1773–1793

L.B LE BEL, Nicolas-Antoine
1804–1845

LC CHARPENTIER, Louis-Joseph
1852, 1854–1879

L.ᵉ LE BEL aîné, Jean-Étienne
1766–1775

LG LE GUAY, Étienne-Charles
1778–1781, 1783–1785, 1808–1840

LG GUÉNEAU, Louis*
1885–1924

LG LE GUAY père, Étienne-Henri
1748–1749, 1751–1796

L.G.

LG LE GRAND, Louis-Antoine
1776–1817

lg LANGLE, Pierre-Jean-Victor-Amable
1837–1845

L.G.ᶜᵉ LANGLACÉ, Jean-Baptiste-Gabriel
1807–1844

L i LIANCE, Antoine-Mathieu*
1754–1777

LLLL. LÉCOT
1773–1802

LM MIREY
1788–1792

LM MIMARD, Louis
1884–1928

P PELUCHE, Léon
1881–1928

LP PARPETTE jeune, Mlle Louise
1794–1798, 1801–1817

LR LAROCHE, de
1759–1802

LR LE RICHE, Josse-François-Joseph*
1757–1801

M MOIRON
1790–1791

M MOYEZ, Jean-Louis
1818–1848

M MICHEL, Ambroise
1772–1780

M MORIN, Jean-Louis
1754–1787

M MASSY
1779–1803

MA MASCRET, Achille
1838–1846

Mas MASCRET, Jean*
1810–1848

MB BUNEL, Mme Marie-Barbe
1778–1816

MₗC — MICAUD, Pierre-Louis
1795–1834

ME *MₗE* — MAUGENDRE*
1879–1887

MₗL — MASCRET, Louis*
1825–1864

m.ₑ — MOYEZ, Pierre*
1827–1848

MₗR — MORIN, Charles-Raphaël
1805–1812

MₑR — MOREAU, Denis-Joseph
1807–1815

M — SOLON, Marc*
1857–1871

N — MORIN
1880–after 1900

N — ALONCLE, François
1758–1781

NB — BESTAULT, Nestor*
1889–1929

ng. — NICQUET
1764–1792

O — OUINT, Émmanuel*
1877–1889

o.ch — OUINT, Charles
1879–1886, 1889–1890

o g — OGER, Jacques-Jean*
1784–1800, 1802–1821

OM — MILET, Optat
1862–1879

P — PINE or PLINE, François-
Bernard-Louis
1854–1870 or later

P — PERROTTIN or PEROTTIN*
1760–1793 or later

P — PARPETTE, Philippe
1755–1757, 1773–1806

P.A. — AVISSE, Alexandre-Paul
1848–1884

PB Pb — BOUCOT, Philippe
1785–1791

P — PIHAN, Charles
1879–1928

J F — FACHARD, Pierre*
1899–1934

P.H. — PHILIPPINE aîné
1778–1791, 1802–1825

P.h. — PHILIPPINE cadet, François
1783–1791, 1801–1839

P.j. — PITHOU jeune
1760–1795

P 7 . P9. — PIERRE jeune, Jean-Jacques
1763–1800

PK — KNIP, Mme de Courcelles
1808–1809, 1817–1826

p.o — PIERRE aîné
1759–1775

P P — PARPETTE aîné, Mlle
1788–1798

R — PERRENOT aîné
1804–1809, 1813–1815

Mark	Name	Dates
PR	ROBERT, Pierre	1813–1832
P.T.	PETIT aîné, Nicolas	1756–1806
St.	PITHOU aîné	1757–1790
R	RITON, Pierre	1821–1860
˙R	SIOUX aîné	1752–1791
R	RICHARD, Nicolas-Joseph	1833–1870 or later
R	ROBERT, Jean-François	1806–1834, 1836–1843
R ...	RICHARD, Pierre	1815–1848
R	GIRARD	1772–1817
R.B.	MAQUERET, Mme	1796–1798, 1817–1820
RB	ROBERT, Jean-François	1806–1843
R	RÉMY, Charles	1886–1897, 1901–1928
RL	ROUSSEL 1758–1774	
R L.		
R	RIOCREUX, Denis-Désiré	1807–1828
Rx	RIOCREUX, Isidore	1846–1849
S	SAMSON, Léon*	1897–1918
S	MÉREAUD aîné, Pierre-Antoine	1754–1791
S	SANDOZ, Alphonse*	1881–1920
Sc	CHANOU, Mlle Sophie, Mme BINET	1779–1798
SD	NOUALHIER, Mme Sophie	1777–1795
S	SIEFFERT, Louis-Eugène	1881–1887, 1894–1898
S.h.	SCHRADRE	1773–1775, 1780–1786
SS	SINSSON or SISSON, Jacques	1795–1846
SSl	SINSSON or SISSON, Louis	1830–1847
SSp	SINSSON or SISSON, Pierre	1818–1848
S. W. Sw	SWEBACH, Jacques-Jose (called FONTAINE)	1803–ca. 1814
T	BINET	1750–1775
C	TROYON, Jean-Marie-Dominique	1801–1817
⊡	TARDY, Claude-Antoine	1755–1795

Latache, Étienne
1870–1879

Fragonard, Théophile
1839–1869

Letourneur*
1756–1762

Trager, Louis
1888–1934

Tristan, Étienne-Joseph
1837–1871, 1879–1882

Villion, Paul*
1886–1934

Vandé, Pierre-Jean-Baptiste
1779–1824

Vandé père
1753–1779

Gérard, Mme, née Vautrin
1781–1802

Vavasseur aîné
1753–1770

Weydinger père
1757–1807

Weydinger second fils, Joseph
1778–1804, 1807–1808, 1811,
1816–1824

Hileken
1769–1774

Hilken (?)
Before 1800

Weydinger troisième fils,
Pierre
1781–1792, 1796–1816

Walter
ca. 1867–ca. 1870

Micaud, Jacques-François
1757–1810

Grison
1749–1771

Catrice
1757–1774

Rocher, Alexandre
1758–1759

Fouré
1749, 1754–1762

Bouillat père, Edmé-
François
1758–1810

Bouillat fils, F.
1800–1811

Joyau
1766–1775

Rosset, Pierre-Joseph
1753–1795

Choisy, Apprien-Julien de
1770–1812

Martinet, Émile-Victor
1847–1878

Le Guay, Pierre-André
1772–1818

Anthaume, Jean-Jacques
1752–1758

Aubert aîné
1754–1758

TARDY, Claude-Antoine
1755–1795

CARDIN
1749–1793 or later

Probably GOMERY or
GOMMERY, Edme 1756–1758

LÉANDRE 1779–1785

ARMAND cadet
1746–1788

GÉNIN, Charles
1756–1757

XHROUET, XHROWET or
SECROIX, Philippe and Mlle
1750–1775

FONTELLIAU, F.
1753–1755

PAJOU
1751–1759

RENARD, Émile
1852–1882

BOUCHER
1754–1762

Probably LEDOUX, Jean-Pierre
1758–1761

BIENFAIT, Jean-Baptiste
1756–after 1770

FRITSCH
1763–1764

BOUCHET, Jean
1763–1793

DUBOIS, Jean-René
1756–1757

SINSSON, SIMPSON or SISSON,
Nicolas
1773–ca. 1800

GAUTIER
1787–1791

BECQUET
1749–1750, 1753–1765

POUILLOT
1773–1778

BUTEUX aîné, Charles
1756–1782

MUTEL
1754–1759, 1765–1766,
1771–1773

ÉVANS, Étienne
1752–1806

YVERNEL
1750–1759

TAILLANDIER or TAILLANDIEZ,
Vincent
1753–1790

BOULANGER fils
1778–1781

CHEVALIER, Pierre-François
1755–1757

THÉVENET père
1741–1777

CORNAILLES, Antoine-
Toussaint
1755–1800

CHULOT, Louis-Gabriel
1755–1800

SIOUX jeune
1752–1759

CAPELLE
1746–1800

BUTEUX fils cadet
1773–1790

DIEU, Jean-Jacques
1777—1790, 1794–1798,
1801–1811

TABARY
1754–1755

CATON
1749–1798

CHAUVEAUX aîné, Michel-
Barnabé
1752–1788

ROCHER, Alexandre
1758–1759

BARDET
1751–1758

FONTAINE, Jacques
1752–1775, 1778–1807

NOËL, Guillaume
1755–1804

RAUX aîné
1766–1779

SIOUX aîné
1752–1791

TANDART jeune, Charles
1756–1760 or TANDART,
Jean-Baptiste
1754–1803

THÉODORE
1765–1771 or later

VIEILLARD aîné
1752–1790

MONGENOT
1754–1764

CARRIÉ or CARRIER
1752–1757

BERTRAND
1757–1774

BERTRAND
1750–1800

BUTEUX fils aîné, Charles-
Nicolas
1763–1801

MÉREAUD jeune, Charles-
Louis
1756–1779

VINCENT jeune
1753–1806

BARRÉ, Louis-Désiré
1846–1881

BIEUVILLE or BIENVILLE
(BIEAUVILLE?), Horace
1879–1925

BRÉCY, Paul* or Henry*
1881–after 1900

COURCY, Alexandre-Frédéric
de
1865–1886

FOURNIER, Anatole
1878–1926

GÉLY, Léopold-Jules-Joseph*
1851–1888

Goupil, Frédéric
1859–1878

Meyer, Alfred
1858–1871

Richard, François
1832–1875

Richard, Émile
1867–1900

Roussel, Paul-Marie
1850–1871

Sandoz, Alphonse*
1881–after 1900

Schilt, Louis-Pierre
1818–1855

III. Nineteenth- and Twentieth-Century Pastes

1. The old hard-paste formula, modified and stabilized by Brongniart at the beginning of the nineteenth century, has remained in continuous use.

2. The original soft-paste formula reappeared in 1849.

3. A new hard paste, invented by the chemists Lauth and Vogt, was launched in 1882. It fired at a lower temperature than the old, and permitted the use of a softer glaze. Because such glaze also fired at a correspondingly lower temperature, it could take advantage of pigments not capable of surviving the earlier kiln temperatures. This technical breakthrough made a new range of colored glazes (*i.e.*, "ground colors") possible. The formula of Lauth and Vogt is still in use.

4. Another distinct ceramic body, called *grosse porcelaine*, or simply *grès*, appeared in 1889.

5. A new soft paste, shown in trial pieces at the Paris Exposition of 1900, was put into production in 1907. Its glaze and decoration compare favorably with those of the *ancien régime*.